The Beginning

Baptism

Body

and Bride

A Local Church Error Refuted !

ISBN: 978-0-9987778-4-9

© copyright J. A. Moorman May, 2017

All Scripture quotes are from the King James Bible except those verses compared and then the source is identified.

And as I began to speak, the Holy Ghost fell on them as on us at the <u>beginning</u>. Acts 11:15.

For as many of you as have been <u>baptised</u> into Christ have put on Christ. Galatians 3:27.

For we are members of his <u>body</u>, of his flesh, and of his bones. Ephesians 5:30.

And the Spirit and the <u>bride</u> say Come. Revelation 22:17.

Address All Inquiries To The Publisher:
Published by:
The Old Paths Publications, Inc.
142 Gold Flume Way
Cleveland, GA 30528
www.theoldpathspublications.com
TOP@theoldpathspublications.com

TABLE OF CONTENTS

4

TABLE OF CONTENTS

INTRODUCTION

The New Testament places great emphasis upon the Local Church. From Acts Two and onward, wherever one looks, in everything from spiritual nurturing to world evangelism, the Local Church is the centre and compass of God's dealings with His people. One would be pressed to find a single example of work or ministry described in the Bible that was independent of the Local Church. It is a great and glorious emphasis, and Independent Baptists have generally been unique in giving it its proper place. They have also been right in showing that while it is Biblical for Local Churches to encourage fellowship with each other, any kind of formal structure *over* the Local Churches in order to maintain that fellowship is unbiblical, becomes cumbersome, distracting, time-consuming and expensive. This of course does not preclude certain ministries which sound Local Churches have banded together to support and which they could little do without, for example Bible and literature publication, Bible Institutes etc.

The Local Church is a glorious New Testament truth, but like all other doctrines it is possible to take it further and make claims for it that the Bible does not make. The late Nineteenth and early Twentieth Centuries saw the rise of *Landmark* Baptist Churches in the USA. J.R. Graves, J.B. Thomas and B.H. Carroll were original exponents. Extreme forms of this movement taught the necessity of baptismal *succession* back to John the Baptist, and that only Baptists who can so trace their own succession are in the Body/Bride of Christ. Among Independent Baptists, there have been less extreme forms, but still maintaining most of the common tenets, among which are the following:

1. Rather than at Pentecost, the Church began at the start of Christ's ministry when He called His disciples.

2. There is no baptism of the Holy Spirit into the spiritual Body of Christ.

3. The "Body of Christ" refers solely to baptised believers in a local church. There is no spiritual Body of Christ to which all believers are joined at conversion.

4. The "Bride of Christ" refers to the inhabitants of the New Jerusalem, rather than the Church today.

These are the views of Dr. Thomas Strouse of Emmanuel Baptist Theological Seminary (EBTS) in Connecticut. Dr. Strouse is a strong defender of the Greek and Hebrew texts underlying the Authorised Version. His teaching materials have been a help to many. He is a friend and ally in the issues that fundamentalists face. On this matter, however, it is believed his views are in error. A number of churches have been influenced, and in more recent times through an extension of EBTS, several churches here in Britain.

Many will, I think, see that the above and further arguments go against the natural sense of Scripture. To grasp them will take some "stretching." Using "the desert island approach", it is not likely that a man alone on an island with only his Bible would come to these conclusions. They are not *naturally* derived and they cannot be *reasonably* sustained or defended. For example, on thirty occasions the Book of Romans declares that the believer is *in Christ*. How can we be *in Christ*, and yet *not* in His Body until baptism and membership in a Local Church? Does, *Know ye not that your bodies are the members of Christ* (I Cor. 6:15), or *he that is joined unto the Lord is one spirit* (I Cor. 6:15), take place at conversion or baptism? Is a pastor really prepared to say to his church and the one he is baptising: "As I raise you from the water, you have now become part of the Body of Christ." One could be excused for wondering if this does not give some kind of a soteriological element to baptism.

We can also be excused for questioning if the basis of the believer's position in Christ is being undermined. As for our standing, from the moment of salvation we are *complete in Christ* (Col. 2:10). Baptism and church membership are essential to our state, experience and outworking of that standing, but do not add a whit to our standing.

This teaching also has a *control* air about it. We are to strongly encourage faithfulness and service in the Local Church, but this goes too far. It crosses the line toward *being lords over God's heritage* (I Pet. 5:3). Rather than the Holy Spirit, it is now the pastor who places the believer in the Body of Christ!!

The common, and we believe Biblical, teaching among fundamental Bible believers is that at conversion we are baptised by the Holy Spirit into spiritual union with Christ. We are *members of His body, of His flesh, and of His bones* (Eph. 5:30). His death has become our death, and His resurrection our resurrection. Believers are in the Body and Bride of Christ. Shortly thereafter we are to manifest our salvation and position in Christ by being baptised in water, and becoming an active member of a Local Church.

In this work, the two basic views are compared. A large number of Scripture passages have been gathered. The view that says the Church began with the calling of the disciples, and which denies a baptism of the Holy Spirit into the Body of Christ, is called here the **Revised Landmark View**. That view which says the Church began at Pentecost, and which believes there is a baptism of the Holy Spirit into the Body of Christ, we call the **Common View**.

The terms, *Revised Landmark* and *Common*, reasonably reflect and identify these two views. The Common View has been generally held by different persuasions of Baptists, and was for example set out in the *Second London Confession* of 1689. Dr. Strouse would likely take exception to his view being called *Revised Landmarkism*. But I think that this is both an accurate and *recognizable* name. Excluding the *chain-link succession*, his teaching contains most of the unique tenets of Landmarkism. When reading his arguments, Landmarkism immediately springs to mind. *Revised Landmarkism* is more precise than his calling it, *Spiritual Kinship*, a term which is little heard of, and likely has a much broader meaning than the view he holds (See *My Church*, p.vi).

CHAPTER 1

Reasons Given In Support of the Revised Landmark View

1. I Corinthians 12:13 refers to water rather than Holy Spirit baptism.

The passage therefore bears no reference to a spiritual Body of Christ. The verse should be translated, "in one spirit are we all baptised into one body"; i.e. "in one spirit of unity (Phil. 1:27), are we all baptised into one local church." The word "spirit" was in the lower case in the 1611 KJV and changed to the upper in the 1769 edition.

Answer:

For a start, it should set warning lights flashing when one has to change the AV translation in order to argue their point. Once an alteration is allowed, (here, a change of case from the instrumental to locative), the door is opened for many others. While generally ἐν will be translated in the locative case, "in", it is translated in the instrumental case "by" (142 times) and "with" (139 times). We will have to let the grammarians comment, but it would certainly seem that as εἰς follows ἐν in the sentence, the instrumental rather than locative is the appropriate usage. Dr Strouse argues that the same construction as I Cor. 12:13 is found in Phil. 1:27 where *the spirit of unity* is meant. But the two passages are different, and there εἰς is not present.

> *For by (ἐν) one Spirit are we all baptized into (εἰς) one body, whether we be Jews or Gentiles,*

11

whether we be bond or free; and have been all made to drink into one Spirit.

Only let your conversation be as it becometh the gospel of Christ: that whether I come and see you, or else be absent, I may hear of your affairs, that ye stand fast in (ἐv) one spirit, with one mind striving together for the faith of the gospel. Phil. 1:27.

The *Spirit* is mentioned seven times in the context of I Cor. 12:13. It is clearly the Holy Spirit in each instance. To make an exception at verse 13, and especially when the verse goes on to say: *and have all been made to drink into one Spirit*, is arbitrary. This concluding part of verse 13 is combined with and defines what is being referred to in the initial statement. It cannot be water in the first part and the Holy Spirit in the second part.

All of the references to "Spirit" in this section were in the lower case in the KJV of 1611; and *all* refer to the Holy Spirit. Interestingly, however, *Holy Ghost* was capitalised, (12:3).

Note the: *we, all, one body* in this passage. If water baptism into the Local Church is the subject, then each of these words are in some sense contradictory. Paul cannot say "we" for he was not water baptised at Corinth. If he does say "we", then it should be: "we were all baptised into a body." If "one" is retained, then it should be: "you were all baptised into one body" etc. The only way these words can be used together is if Holy Spirit baptism into the spiritual Body of Christ is the subject.

Though taking the opposite view, Dr. Strouse admits: "Certainly the context would favor *pneuma* being the Divine Spirit." (*My Church*, p.150).

*7 But **the manifestation of the Spirit** is given to every man to profit withal. 8 For to one is given by **the Spirit** the word of wisdom; to another the word of knowledge by **the same Spirit**; 9 To another faith by **the same Spirit**; to another the gifts of healing by **the same Spirit**; 10 To another the working of miracles; to another prophecy; to another discerning of spirits; to another divers kinds of tongues; to another the interpretation of tongues: 11 But all these worketh **that one and the selfsame Spirit**, dividing to every man severally as **he** will. 12 For as the body is one, and hath many members, and all the members of that one body, being many, are one body: so also is Christ. 13 For **by one Spirit** are we all baptized into one body, whether we be Jews or Gentiles, whether we be bond or free; and have been all made to drink **into one Spirit**.... 18 But now hath God set the members every one of them in the body, as it hath pleased him.... 24 For our comely parts have no need: but God hath tempered the body together, having given more abundant honour to that part which lacked. 25 That there should be no schism in the body; but that the members should have the same care one for another. 26 And whether one member suffer, all the members suffer with it; or one member be honoured, all the members rejoice with it. 27 Now ye are the body of Christ, and members in particular. 28 And God hath set some in the church, first apostles, secondarily prophets, thirdly teachers, after that miracles, then gifts of healings, helps,* *governments, diversities of tongues.* I Cor.12:7-13, 18, 24-28.

In a parallel passage, it is the Gospel and not water baptism that places us into the Body of Christ.

That the Gentiles should be fellowheirs, and of the <u>same body</u>, and partakers of his promise in Christ <u>by the gospel</u>. Eph. 3:6.

2. Passages in the Epistles thought formerly to refer to Holy Spirit baptism into Christ, refer instead to water baptism into the Local Church.

In the Gospels it is said that Christ will baptise with the Holy Spirit, while the Epistles speak of the believer being baptised into (unto) Christ. This difference of agency shows that the two actions are different, with the latter referring to water baptism.

Answer:

The Gospels (with Acts) and Epistles describe two aspects of the same action within the Godhead. From Pentecost onward, Christ by the Holy Spirit baptises believers into His own spiritual Body. When read in their context, the Epistle passages are shown clearly to <u>extend beyond</u> water baptism. These passages must refer to Holy Spirit baptism into Christ. They reveal the spiritual reality of our union with Christ of which water baptism is the outward picture. These passages describe the basis of a believer's victory over sin. In Romans 3-5, Christ died *for* us, but in Romans 6-8 we died *with* Christ, and are *in* Christ. To make them refer solely to water takes away the chief basis of the believer's position and victory in Christ.

Christ the Baptiser

I indeed baptize you with water unto repentance: but he that cometh after me is mightier than I, whose shoes I am not worthy to bear: **he shall baptize you with the Holy Ghost**, *and with fire.* Mt. 3:11.

And I knew him not: but he that sent me to baptize with water, the same said unto me, Upon whom thou shalt see the Spirit descending, and remaining on him, the same is **he which baptizeth with the Holy Ghost**. Jhn. 1:33.

For John truly baptized with water; but **ye shall be baptized with the Holy Ghost** *not many days hence.* Acts 1:5.

1 And when the day of Pentecost was fully come, they were all with one accord in one place. 2 And suddenly there came a sound from heaven as of a rushing mighty wind, and it filled all the house where they were sitting. 3 And there appeared unto them cloven tongues like as of fire, and it sat upon each of them. 4 And they were all filled with the Holy Ghost, and began to speak with other tongues, as the Spirit gave them utterance. Acts 2:1-4.

Therefore being by the right hand of God exalted, and having received of the Father the promise of the Holy Ghost, he hath shed forth this, which ye now see and hear. Acts 2:33.

15 And as I began to speak, the Holy Ghost fell on them, as on us at the beginning. 16 Then remembered I the word of the Lord, how that he said,

15

*John indeed baptized with water; but **ye shall be baptized with the Holy Ghost**.* Acts 11:15,16.

Baptised into Christ

*3 Know ye not, that so many of us as were **baptized into Jesus Christ** were **baptized into his death**? 4 Therefore we are **buried with him by baptism into death**: that like as Christ was raised up from the dead by the glory of the Father, even so we also should walk in newness of life. 5 For if we have been planted together in the likeness of his death, we shall be also in the likeness of his resurrection: 6 Knowing this, that <u>our old man is crucified with him</u>, that the body of sin might be destroyed, that henceforth we should not serve sin.* Rom. 6:3-6.

*For **by one Spirit are we all baptized into one body**, whether we be Jews or Gentiles, whether we be bond or free; and <u>have been all made to drink into one Spirit</u>.* I Cor. 12:13.

*26 For ye are all the children of God <u>by faith</u> in Christ Jesus. 27 For **as many of you as have been baptized into Christ** <u>have put on Christ</u>. 28 There is neither Jew nor Greek, there is neither bond nor free, there is neither male nor female: for ye are all one in Christ Jesus. 29 And if ye be Christ's, then are ye Abraham's seed, and heirs according to the promise.* Gal. 3:26-29.

9 For in him dwelleth all the fulness of the Godhead bodily. 10 And ye are <u>complete in him, which is the head</u> of all principality and power: 11 In whom also ye are <u>circumcised with the circumcision made without hands</u>, in putting off the body of the

16

sins of the flesh by the circumcision of Christ: 12 ***Buried with him in baptism****, <u>wherein also ye are risen with him through the faith of the operation of God</u>, who hath raised him from the dead. 13 And you, being dead in your sins and the uncircumcision of your flesh, hath he <u>quickened together with him</u>, having forgiven you all trespasses.* Col. 2:9-13.

The underlined statements in these last four passages go far beyond water baptism.

> *our old man is crucified with him*
>
> *have been all made to drink into one Spirit*
>
> *have put on Christ*
>
> *complete in him*
>
> *circumcised with the circumcision made without hands*
>
> *risen with him through the faith of the operation of God*

Other passages amplify this:

> *Know ye not that your bodies are the members of Christ?* (I Cor. 6:15).
>
> *But he that is joined unto the Lord is one spirit.* (I Cor. 6:17).

It is a shallow and spiritually harmful interpretation that relegates these verses only to water baptism.

3. The "Body of Christ" is solely a Local Church term.

It refers exclusively to immersed believers in a Local Church. Apart from water baptism and the Local Church, a believer is not in the Body of Christ.

Answer:

The Bible presents *the Body of Christ* as a singular term. We read of Churches and the Church, but never the Body and Bodies. It is never in the plural. The Head is One; the Body is One. The idea of many Bodies of Christ does not rest well. Nor does Dr. Strouse relieve this unease when he asks and answers:

How then can Christ be the head of many bodies? He can because He is omnipresent. (Notes, p.7).

Scripture repeatedly says *the body is* <u>*one*</u>. Therefore in its primary sense we see that all believers are *in* and *joined to* Christ. The *Body of Christ* refers to Christ Himself, and those who are His by redemption. As such, however, we would expect that those who are in His Body to manifest this by conforming to the Biblical pattern and become active members of Local Churches. Therefore application of this term can, as in I Corinthians 12:27, be made to the Local Church; but in its primary sense the term clearly goes beyond this.

And believers were the more <u>added to the Lord</u>, multitudes both of men and women. Acts 5:14.

For he was a good man, and full of the Holy Ghost and of faith: and much people was <u>added unto the Lord</u>. Acts 11:24.

*4 For as <u>we</u> have many members in **one body**, and all members have not the same office: 5 So <u>we</u>, being many, are **one body in Christ**, and every one members one of another.* Rom. 12:4,5.

15 Know ye not that <u>your bodies are the members of Christ</u>? shall I then take the members of Christ, and make them the members of an harlot? God forbid. 16 What? know ye not that he which is joined to an harlot is one body? for two, saith he, shall be one flesh. 17 But <u>he that is joined unto the Lord is one spirit</u>. I Cor. 6:15-17.

*For <u>we</u> being many are one bread, and **one body**: for <u>we</u> are all partakers of that <u>one bread</u>.* I Cor. 10:17.

*12 For <u>as the body is one</u>, and hath many members, and all the members of that one body, being many, are **one body**: <u>so also is Christ</u>. 13 For by one Spirit are <u>we</u> all baptized into **one body**, whether we be Jews or Gentiles, whether we be bond or free; <u>and have been all made to drink into one Spirit</u>.* I Cor. 12:12,13.

*Now ye are **the body of Christ**, and members in particular.* I Cor. 12:27.

For as many of you as have been baptized into Christ <u>have put on Christ</u>. Gal. 3:27.

*22 And hath put all things under his feet, and gave him to be <u>the head</u> over all things to <u>the church</u>, 23 Which is **his body**, the fulness of him that filleth all in all.* Eph. 1:22,23.

19

And that he might reconcile both unto God in **one body** _by the cross_, *having slain the enmity thereby.* Eph. 2:16.

That the Gentiles should be fellowheirs, and of **the same body**, *and partakers of his promise in Christ* _by the gospel_. Eph. 3:6. [Note: We enter the Body by the Cross and by the Gospel, not baptism].

There is **one body**, *and* _one Spirit_, *even as ye are called in* _one hope_ *of your calling.* Eph. 4:4.

From whom **the whole body** *fitly joined together and compacted by that which every joint supplieth, according to the effectual working in the measure of every part, maketh increase of* **the body** *unto the edifying of itself in love.* Eph. 4:16.

For the husband is the head of the wife, even as Christ is the head of the church: and he is the saviour of **the body**. Eph. 5:23.

And not holding the Head, from which **all the body** *by joints and bands having nourishment ministered, and knit together, increaseth with the increase of God.* Col. 2:19.

1 _I am the true vine_, and my Father is the husbandman. 2 _Every branch in me_ that beareth not fruit he taketh away: and every branch that beareth fruit, he purgeth it, that it may bring forth more fruit. 3 Now ye are clean through the word which I have spoken unto you. 4 _Abide in me, and I in you_. As the branch cannot bear fruit of itself, except it abide in the vine; no more can ye, except ye abide in me. 5 _I am the vine, ye are the branches_: He that abideth in me, and I in him, the same bringeth forth much fruit: for without me ye can do nothing. Jhn. 15:1-5.

And, notice especially:

*For we are members of **his body**, of his flesh, and of his bones.* Eph. 5:30.

How, as the Scriptures repeatedly state, could we be *in* Christ, if not in His spiritual Body? Is it only after water baptism and church membership that He becomes our Head and we are placed in His Body? Scripture makes the plain statement that *we are members of **his body**, of his flesh, and of his bones.* (Eph. 5:30). Water baptism and the local church should picture this, but are the *effect* not the *cause.*

Under Section III, *Post Pentecost Names Given to the Church*, a full list is given of the "Body" passages. There we also discuss the misnomer, "Universal Church."

4. The "Bride of Christ" refers to New Jerusalem and its inhabitants rather than the Church today.

Both OT and NT saints will inhabit New Jerusalem. The city is specifically called *the Bride* in Revelation 21:2,9. Dr. Strouse's material as far as I can see does not refer any of the Bride passages in the Gospels and Epistles to the Church today. In this he seems to follow B. H. Carroll's *prospective* view of Eph. 5:23-32 (See Carroll, *Ecclesia – The Church,* p.6). Thus, there is not an actual Bride of Christ until New Jerusalem appears.

Answer:

As with the Body passages, Landmark Baptists have sought to show that the Bride of Christ is also a solely Local Church term. However, for others, while "many bodies" may to them be a manageable concept; "many brides" is not! The "Bride" passages in the Gospels and Epistles harmonize with the spiritual Body of Christ, but as this latter is rejected; the so-called prospective view must be appealed to. The flaw with this is that the verbs in Ephesians 5: 23-32 are in the present tense. There is therefore a Bride of Christ *Today*.

If no reference is made to a Bride of Christ apart from New Jerusalem: Whose wedding is taking place in Revelation 19:7-9, and Who says *Come* in Revelation 22:17?

> *For I am jealous over you with godly jealousy: for I have espoused you to one husband, that I may present you as* **a chaste virgin to Christ***. II Cor. 11:2.*

> *23 For the husband is the head of the wife, even as Christ is the head of the church: and he is the saviour of the body. 24 Therefore as the church is subject unto Christ, so let the wives be to their own husbands in every thing. 25 Husbands, love your wives, even as Christ also loved the church, and gave himself for it; 26 That he might sanctify and cleanse it with the washing of water by the word, 27 That he might present it to himself a glorious church, not having spot, or wrinkle, or any such thing; but that it should be holy and without blemish. 28 So ought men to love their wives as their own bodies. He that loveth his wife loveth himself. 29 For no man ever yet hated his own flesh; but nourisheth and cherisheth it, even as the Lord the church: 30 For we are members of his body, of his flesh, and of his bones. 31 For this cause shall a man leave his father*

and mother, and shall be joined unto his wife, and they two shall be one flesh. 32 <u>This is a great mystery: but I speak concerning Christ and the church</u>. Eph. 5:23-32.

7 Let us be glad and rejoice, and give honour to him: for <u>the marriage of the Lamb</u> is come, and his wife hath made herself ready. 8 And to her was granted that she should be arrayed in fine linen, clean and white: for the fine linen is the righteousness of saints. 9 And he saith unto me, Write, Blessed are they which are called unto <u>the marriage supper of the Lamb</u>. And he saith unto me, These are the true sayings of God. Rev. 19: 7-9.

*And I John saw the holy city, new Jerusalem, coming down from God out of heaven, prepared as **a bride** adorned for her husband.* Rev. 21:2.

*And there came unto me one of the seven angels which had the seven vials full of the seven last plagues, and talked with me, saying, Come hither, I will shew thee **the bride, the Lamb's wife**.* Rev. 21:9.

*And the Spirit and **the bride** say, Come. And let him that heareth say, Come. And let him that is athirst come. And whosoever will, let him take the water of life freely.* Rev. 22:17.

Old Testament saints will also dwell in New Jerusalem (Heb. 11:10), but the emphasis must be that this is the dwelling place of the Bride, the Church. Note that the Bride, because of the marriage (19:7-9), is also the Wife. The *Bride* speaks of beauty and bliss, the *Wife* of permanence. Throughout the present dispensation it is the Bride not the Old Testament saints, who say, *Come*. All of this is in contrast with that other woman described in Revelation 17: *The Harlot* – the false church.

5. The Church began with the call of the disciples in Mark 3:13-19.

This is a key plank of Landmarkism. Christ's calling of the disciples was the beginning of His called out assembly. In this we see the "budding" of the church. A bud contains within itself all the fullness of the mature form, and during the Christ's ministry those things that were essential to compose a church, were present. (See: Davis W. Huckabee, *Studies in Church Truth*, vol. 1, p.23).

Answer:

Indeed, the disciples would later become the Church. But Scripture does not call this gathering in Mark 3 a Church. It does not give the impression of it being a Church. No emphasis is made of people being urged to join this "Church." It was as Scripture shows, *a call of the Twelve to follow Christ.* For the many reasons given below, the Church was yet to come.

> *13 And he goeth up into a mountain, and calleth unto him whom he would: and they came unto him. 14 And he ordained twelve, that they should be with him, and that he might send them forth to preach, 15 And to have power to heal sicknesses, and to cast out devils: 16 And Simon he surnamed Peter; 17 And James the son of Zebedee, and John the brother of James; and he surnamed them Boanerges, which is, The sons of thunder: 18 And Andrew, and Philip, and Bartholomew, and Matthew, and Thomas, and James the son of Alphaeus, and*

> *Thaddaeus, and Simon the Canaanite, 19 And Judas
> Iscariot, which also betrayed him: and they went into
> an house.* Mk. 3:13-19.

Some refer to the early gatherings of the disciples
as an embryo or a seed. But, an embryo and seed must
have a birth. And in fact, regarding seed, and to follow the
Scripture analogy, there must be *death* or it *will abide
alone!* The church could only begin after Calvary.

> *21 The same came therefore to Philip, which
> was of Bethsaida of Galilee, and desired him, saying,
> Sir, we would see Jesus. 22 Philip cometh and telleth
> Andrew: and again Andrew and Philip tell Jesus. 23
> And Jesus answered them, saying, The hour is come,
> that the Son of man should be glorified. 24 Verily,
> verily, I say unto you, Except a corn of wheat fall
> into the ground and die, it abideth alone: but if it die,
> it bringeth forth much fruit.* Jhn. 12:21-24.

If this call and gathering constituted a Church, we
would expect the Bible to say so. It does not. Very few,
unaware of the Landmark teaching, in reading through the
four Gospels, would ever suspect that they were reading
about a Local Church.

6. Matthew 16:18 means: "Upon this rock I will *build up* an already existing Church."

As the Church began with the call of the disciples,
Matthew 16:18 is not a promise of a future beginning, but
rather that Christ will continue to build up, strengthen, and
establish what was already in existence. The word
oikodomeo is translated "built up" (once) in I Pet. 2:5, and
"edify" in seven other passages. This is the meaning of
Matthew 16:18.

Answer:

This is simply not the impression given in the words: *upon this rock I will build my church*. The future tense is used here and throughout the passage. The mention of *the rock* upon which the structure is going to be built (referring to Peter's profession that *Christ is the Son of the Living God*) points naturally to a building project not as yet begun.

The statement can hardly allow for a *previous* "building project." Christ does not say, "I will continue to build my church." It would be highly unusual to speak of building up and strengthening an edifice that had not been previously mentioned. This is the first mention of the Church.

The promise of Matthew 16:18 is given *near the end* of Christ's earthly ministry. Up until now, there is no indication in John the Baptist's or our Lord's ministry of a call to become part of a Local Church. Further, the Church is said to be a *mystery* (Eph. 3:1-9). It was not revealed until now.

By pointing to the foundation, *the rock*, rather than a supposed superstructure, Christ shows that the superstructure was not then in existence. That Christ's promise follows immediately upon Peter's declaration shows clearly that this declaration is the *rock* upon which the Church will be built. There were previous declarations but none so full as this. At the end of His ministry Christ identifies what the foundation of the Church will be: *Thou art the Christ, the Son of the living God.*

Here for the second time an appeal is made for a possible AV alteration. It is fine as it is! In some thirty

26

instances *oikodomeo* is translated as Matthew 16:18. It is never translated "edify" in the Gospels. The other occurrences in Matthew give an identical meaning as 16:18.

> 7:24 *a wise man, which built his house upon a rock*
>
> 7:26 *a foolish man, which built his house upon the sand*
>
> 21:33 *a certain householder, which…built a tower*
>
> 21:42 *The stone which the builders rejected*
>
> 23:29 *ye build the tombs of the prophets*
>
> 26:61 *I am able to destroy the temple of God, and to build it in three days*
>
> 27:40 *Thou that destroyest the temple, and buildest it in three days*

There are seven statements in Matthew 16:18-19 showing future action. None assume past or present action.

> *15 He saith unto them, But whom say ye that I am? 16 And Simon Peter answered and said, Thou art the Christ, the Son of the living God. 17 And Jesus answered and said unto him, Blessed art thou, Simon Barjona: for flesh and blood hath not revealed it unto thee, but my Father which is in heaven. 18 And I say also unto thee, That thou art Peter, and*

(1) *upon this rock I will build my church; and*
(2) *the gates of hell shall not prevail against it. 19 And*
(3) *I will give unto thee the keys of the kingdom of heaven: and*
(4) *whatsoever thou shalt bind on earth*
(5) *shall be bound in heaven: and*
(6) *whatsoever thou shalt loose on earth*
(7) *shall be loosed in heaven.* Mt. 16:15-19.

7. Christ sang in the church at the Last Supper.

Hebrews 2:12 refers to the Last Supper; therefore the Church was already in existence.

Answer:

This is another example of how "stretched" the arguments become. In both Hebrews 2:9-12 and Psalm 22:16-22 our Lord's singing is shown to be *after* His work on the Cross. And, as Psalm 22:25-28 shows, it clearly looks forward to the Millennium.

> *And* **when they had sung an hymn**, *they went out into the mount of Olives.* Mt. 26:30.

> *9 But we see Jesus, who was made a little lower than the angels for* <u>*the suffering of death*</u>, *crowned with glory and honour; that he by the grace of God should taste death for every man. 10 For it became him, for whom are all things, and by whom are all things, in bringing many sons unto glory, to make the captain of their salvation perfect through sufferings. 11 For both he that sanctifieth and they who are sanctified are all of one: for which cause he is not ashamed to call them brethren, 12 Saying, I will declare thy name unto my brethren,* **in the midst**

28

of the church will I sing praise unto thee. Heb. 2:9-12.

16 For dogs have compassed me: the assembly of the wicked have inclosed me: they pierced my hands and my feet. 17 I may tell all my bones: they look and stare upon me. 18 They part my garments among them, and cast lots upon my vesture. 19 But be not thou far from me, O LORD: O my strength, haste thee to help me. 20 Deliver my soul from the sword; my darling from the power of the dog. 21 Save me from the lion's mouth: for thou hast heard me from the horns of the unicorns. 22 I will declare thy name unto my brethren: **in the midst of the congregation will I praise thee.** Psa. 22:16-22.

25 **My praise shall be of thee in the great congregation**: *I will pay my vows before them that fear him. 26 The meek shall eat and be satisfied: they shall praise the LORD that seek him: your heart shall live for ever. 27 All the ends of the world shall remember and turn unto the LORD: and all the kindreds of the nations shall worship before thee. 28 For the kingdom is the LORD's: and he is the governor among the nations.* Psa. 22:25-28.

8. "Added to the church daily" (Acts 2:47) indicates the church was already in existence.

Answer:

If that were the case, why do we not read about this "adding" before the Day of Pentecost? Prior to verse 41, there is no statement in the Gospels of people being *added* to anything. Verse 47 records the first time that an assembled gathering is called a church. Notice that *daily* (verse 47) follows *the same day* (Pentecost, verse 41). Notice also, Pentecost is called a *beginning* (Acts 11:15). Acts 1 describes a gathering, but it was not called a Church.

> *41 Then <u>they that gladly received his word were baptized: and the same day there were</u> **added unto them** about three thousand souls. 42 And they continued stedfastly in the apostles' doctrine and fellowship, and in breaking of bread, and in prayers. 43 And fear came upon every soul: and many wonders and signs were done by the apostles. 44 And all that believed were together, and had all things common; 45 And sold their possessions and goods, and parted them to all men, as every man had need. 46 And they, continuing <u>daily</u> with one accord in the temple, and breaking bread from house to house, did eat their meat with gladness and singleness of heart, 47 Praising God, and having favour with all the people. And <u>the Lord</u> **added to the church** <u>daily such as should be saved</u>. Acts 2:41-47.*

And as I began to speak, the Holy Ghost fell on them as on us at the <u>beginning</u>. Acts 11:15.

9. According to Mark 13:34, Christ left His house (the church) when He ascended back to heaven.

This *house* refers to the Local Church. This name is given to the Church both before and after Pentecost.

Answer:

In the Gospels, a "house" is shown to refer to Israel, the temple, and heaven. In the Epistles there are seven instances where the church is called a *house*, and also several places where it is called a *household*. There is, however, no clear instance of this identification in the Gospels. Further, Mark 13:34 is a parable: *as a man taking a far journey, who left his house*.

> *33 Take ye heed, watch and pray: for ye know not when the time is. 34 For <u>the Son of Man is as a man taking a far journey, who left</u> **his house**, and gave authority to his servants, and to every man his work, and commanded the porter to watch. 35 Watch ye therefore: for ye know not when <u>the master of the</u> **house** cometh, at even, or at midnight, or at the cockcrowing, or in the morning. Mk. 13:33-35.*

> *But go rather to the lost sheep of **the house of Israel**. Mt. 10:6.*

> *It is enough for the disciple that he be as his master, and the servant as his lord. If they have called the <u>master of the</u> **house** Beelzebub, how much more shall they call them of **his household**? Mt. 10:25.*

> *How he entered into **the house of God**, and did eat the shewbread, which was not lawful for him to eat, neither for them which were with him, but only for the priests? Mt. 12:4.*

> *43 When the unclean spirit is gone out of a man, he walketh through dry places, seeking rest, and findeth none. 44 Then he saith, I will return into **my house** from whence I came out; and when he is come, he findeth it empty, swept, and garnished. Mt. 12:43-44.*

*But he answered and said, I am not sent but unto the lost sheep of **the house of Israel**.* Mt. 15:24.

*And said unto them, It is written, **My house** shall be called **the house of prayer**; but ye have made it a den of thieves.* Mt. 21:13.

*37 O Jerusalem, Jerusalem, thou that killest the prophets, and stonest them which are sent unto thee, how often would I have gathered thy children together, even as a hen gathereth her chickens under her wings, and ye would not! 38 Behold, **your house** is left unto you desolate. 39 For I say unto you, Ye shall not see me henceforth, till ye shall say, Blessed is he that cometh in the name of the Lord.* Mt. 23:37-38.

*To a virgin espoused to a man whose name was Joseph, of **the house of David**; and the virgin's name was Mary.* Lk. 1:27.

*And he shall reign over **the house of Jacob** for ever; and of his kingdom there shall be no end.* Lk. 1:33.

*And Joseph also went up from Galilee, out of the city of Nazareth, into Judaea, unto the city of David, which is called Bethlehem; (because he was of **the house and lineage of David**.* Lk. 2:4.

*21 So that servant came, and shewed his lord these things. Then the master of **the house** being angry said to his servant, Go out quickly into the streets and lanes of the city, and bring in hither the poor, and the maimed, and the halt, and the blind. 22 And the servant said, Lord, it is done as thou hast commanded, and yet there is room.*

32

*23 And the lord said unto the servant, Go out into the highways and hedges, and compel them to come in, that **my house** may be filled.* Lk. 14:21-23.

*And his disciples remembered that it was written, The zeal of **thine house** hath eaten me up.* Jhn. 2:17.

*And the servant abideth not in **the house** for ever: but the Son abideth ever.* Jhn. 8:35.

*In **my Father's house** are many mansions: if it were not so, I would have told you. I go to prepare a place for you.* Jhn. 14:2.

*And suddenly there came a sound from heaven as of a rushing mighty wind, and it filled **all the house** where they were sitting.* Acts 2:2.

*Therefore let all **the house of Israel** know assuredly, that God hath made the same Jesus, whom ye have crucified, both Lord and Christ.* Acts 2:36.

10. As the pre-existing Tabernacle and Temple were filled with the glory of God, so the pre-existing Church was filled with the Holy Spirit at Pentecost.

The Tabernacle and Temple were first constructed and then filled. David gathered, Solomon built, and Gods glory then filled the Temple. So John the Baptist gathered, Christ built, and the Church was filled with the Holy Spirit on the Day of Pentecost.

Answer:

This is an attractive analogy, but the Gospels do not describe the ministries of John and our Lord being a

33

call to become part of a Local Church. Consistently throughout the Gospels theirs was a call to *repent for the kingdom of heaven was at hand* (Mt. 3:1; 4:17; cp. 16:21). There is a huge amount of Scripture given to the construction of the Tabernacle and Temple prior to the glory coming down and filling the edifice. Nothing remotely like this is apparent in the Gospels for a pre-existing Church.

11. The Common View is based on Plato's philosophy.

> "In his thinking, each man had a 'soul' which was part of the universal Oversoul....One of the errors of the Patristics [Church Fathers], perhaps unbeknownst to them, was to embrace Platonic philosophy and read into Christian Scripture the doctrine of *catholicity*." (*My Church*, pp. 54,55).

Answer:

This is an unworthy aspersion. The Common View is based *solely* on Scripture. It is drawn *naturally* from Scripture. There was not some latent behind the scenes influence causing us to see this. We certainly were not "unbeknownst" influenced by Plato. Including myself, I doubt if one in ten thousand Independent Baptists has ever heard of Plato's Oversoul.

CHAPTER 2

Reasons Given In Support of the Common View

Again, only with the greatest effort can the eleven arguments listed be defended. Unless a person is "pre-programmed" very few would guess that a single one of these was taught in the Bible. The arguments are forced, unnatural, arbitrary. Neither alone nor in combination can they be *reasonably* sustained. With the Common View, it is different.

1. Gatherings in the Gospels were not called a "Church."

It is rarely before, but frequently after Pentecost that we find the word "Church." *It is mentioned 3 times before, and 106 times after.* This word is not found in Mark, Luke or John. It is mentioned in Matthew near the end of Christ's teaching ministry and clearly in *prospect* (16:18: 18:17 twice). A normal reading of the Gospels does not give the impression that the disciples in their following Christ constituted a church gathering. If it were a church, we would expect the Scriptures to call it so. <u>The first time an assembled gathering is called a church is in Acts 2:47</u>.

> *Praising God, and having favour with all the people. And the Lord added to the **church** <u>daily</u> such as should be saved.*

2. The Church is said to be yet future in the Gospels.

Some seven months before going to the Cross, Christ said, I *will* build my church. He also gave instructions as to what *will* and *shall* be done if a dispute arose in the soon to be formed church. The verbs speak of an event still to come. As shown above, nothing is said about building the Church prior to this.

> *And I say also unto thee, That thou art Peter, and upon this rock I **will** build my church; and the gates of hell **shall not** prevail against it.* Mt. 16:18.

> *16 But if he **will not** hear thee, then take with thee one or two more, that in the mouth of two or three witnesses every word may be established. 17 And if he **shall** neglect to hear them, tell it unto the church: but if he neglect to hear the church, let him be unto thee as an heathen man and a publican.* Mt. 18:16,17.

3. Christ is the Head of the Church.

It is after, and in virtue of His resurrection and ascension that Christ is said to have assumed this title.

> *And he is the **head** of the <u>body</u>, the <u>church</u>: who is the beginning, <u>the firstborn from the dead</u>; that in all things he might have the preeminence.* Col. 1:18.

> *19 And what is the exceeding greatness of his power to us-ward who believe, according to the working of his mighty power, 20 Which he wrought in Christ, <u>when he raised him from the dead</u>, and <u>set him at his own right hand</u> in the heavenly places, 21*

*Far above all principality, and power, and might, and dominion, and every name that is named, not only in this world, but also in that which is to come: 22 And hath put all things under his feet, and gave him to be the **head** over all things to the <u>church</u>, 23 Which is his <u>body</u>, the fulness of him that filleth all in all.* Eph. 1:19-23.

*But speaking the truth in love, may grow up into him in all things, which is the **head**, even Christ.* Eph. 4:15.

*For the husband is the head of the wife, even as Christ is the **head** of the <u>church</u>: and he is the saviour of the <u>body</u>.* Eph. 5:23.

*And not holding the **Head**, from which all the <u>body</u> by joints and bands having nourishment ministered, and knit together, increaseth with the increase of God.* Col. 2:19.

4. The Church is called the Church of the Firstborn.

Colossians 1:18 links this term to the Resurrection. Therefore, there was no Church before.

*To the general assembly and **church of the firstborn**, which are written in heaven, and to God the Judge of all, and to the spirits of just men made perfect.* Heb. 12:23.

*15 Who is the image of the invisible God, **the firstborn of every creature**: 16 For by him were all things created, that are in heaven, and that are in earth, visible and invisible, whether they be thrones,* *or dominions, or principalities, or powers: all things were created by him, and for him: 17 And he is before all things, and by him all things consist. 18 And he is the <u>head of the body, the church</u>: who is the beginning, **the firstborn from the dead**; that in all things he might have the preeminence.* Col. 1:15-18.

God hath fulfilled the same unto us their children, in that <u>he hath raised up Jesus again</u>; as it is also written in the second psalm, Thou art my Son, <u>this day have I begotten thee</u>. Acts 13:33.

*For whom he did foreknow, he also did predestinate to be conformed to the image of his Son, that he might be **the firstborn among many brethren**.* Rom. 8:29.

*3 Who being the brightness of his glory, and the express image of his person, and upholding all things by the word of his power, when he had by himself <u>purged our sins</u>, sat down on the right hand of the Majesty on high: 4 Being made so much better than the angels, as he hath by inheritance obtained a more excellent name than they. 5 For unto which of the angels said he at any time, Thou art my Son, **this day have I begotten thee**? And again, I will be to him a Father, and he shall be to me a Son? 6 And again, when he bringeth in **the firstbegotten** into the world, he saith, And let all the angels of God worship him.* Heb. 1:3-6.

5. The Church could not begin until the baptizing work of the Holy Spirit.

Acts 1:5 shows that this took place on the Day of Pentecost. Thereafter believers are baptised, joined, and placed in the spiritual Body of Christ. *We are members of his body, of His flesh, and of His bones.* Eph. 5:30. See point 3 above.

> *For John truly baptized with water; but ye shall be **baptized with the Holy Ghost** not many days hence.* Acts 1:5. See Acts 11:15-17.

> *For by one Spirit are we all **baptized into one body**, whether we be Jews or Gentiles, whether we be bond or free; and have been all made to drink into one Spirit.* I Cor. 12:13.

> *3 Know ye not, that so many of us as were **baptized into Jesus Christ** were **baptized into his death**? 4 Therefore we are **buried with him by baptism into death**: that like as Christ was raised up from the dead by the glory of the Father, even so we also should walk in newness of life. 5 For if we have been planted together in the likeness of his death, we shall be also in the likeness of his resurrection: 6 Knowing this, that our old man is crucified with him, that the body of sin might be destroyed, that henceforth we should not serve sin.* Rom. 6:3-6.

> *For as many of you as have been **baptized into Christ** have put on Christ.* Gal. 3:27.

> ***Buried with him in baptism**, wherein also ye are risen with him through the faith of the operation of God, who hath raised him from the dead.* Col. 2:12.

*I am **crucified with Christ**: neverthless I live; yet not I, but Christ liveth in me: and the life which I now live in the flesh I live by the faith of the Son of God, who loved me, and gave himself for me.* Gal. 2:20.

*What? know ye not that your body is the temple of **the Holy Ghost which is in you**, which ye have of God, and ye are not your own?* I Cor. 6:19.

*To whom God would make known what is the riches of the glory of this mystery among the Gentiles; which is **Christ in you**, the hope of glory.* Col. 1:27.

Note: The baptism of Ephesians 4:5 is likely to be the baptism of Luke 12:50 and Matt. 20:22. (The baptism of Calvary's Cross), of which Spirit baptism is the *effect* and water baptism the *picture*.

*4 There is <u>one body</u>, and one Spirit, even as ye are called in one hope of your calling; 5 One Lord, one faith, **one baptism**.* Eph. 4:4,5.

*But **I have a baptism to be baptized with**; and how am I straitened till it be accomplished!* Lk. 12:50.

*But Jesus answered and said, Ye know not what ye ask. Are ye able to drink of the cup that I shall drink of, and **to be baptized with the baptism that I am baptized with**? They say unto him, We are able.* Mt. 20:22.

6. There is a *ye in Me* and *I in you* relationship between Christ and the believer.

It is because of the baptism of the Holy Spirit that believers are said to be *in* Christ. This is not a pre Pentecost experience. One could not say *I am crucified with Christ*, and *Christ liveth in me* (Gal. 2:20), before the death and resurrection of Christ. Repeatedly the Epistles tell us that we are *in Christ*, therefore *we are members of his body, of his flesh, and of his bones* (Eph. 5:30). Notice in the following the change from the future (in John) to the present (in the Epistles).

At that day ye shall know that I am in my Father, and ye in me, and I in you. Jhn. 14:20.

Jesus answered and said unto him, If a man love me, he will keep my words: and my Father will love him, and we will come unto him, and make our abode with him. Jhn. 14:23.

I in them, and thou in me, that they may be made perfect in one; and that the world may know that thou hast sent me, and hast loved them, as thou hast loved me. Jhn. 17:23.

And if Christ be in you, the body is dead because of sin; but the Spirit is life because of righteousness. Rom. 8:10.

7 Salute Andronicus and Junia, my kinsmen, and my fellow-prisoners, who are of note among the apostles, who also were in Christ before me. 8 Greet Amplias my beloved in the Lord. 9 Salute Urbane, our helper in Christ, and Stachys my beloved. 10 Salute Apelles approved in Christ. Salute them which are of Aristobulus' household. Rom. 16:7-10.

43

*For as in Adam all die, even so **in Christ** shall all be made alive.* I Cor. 15:22.

*Therefore if any man be **in Christ**, he is a new creature: old things are passed away; behold, all things are become new.* II Cor. 5:17.

*I am crucified with Christ: neverthless I live; yet not I, but **Christ liveth in me**: and the life which I now live in the flesh I live by the faith of the Son of God, who loved me, and gave himself for me.* Gal. 2:20.

*To the praise of the glory of his grace, wherein he hath made us accepted **in the beloved**.* Eph. 1:6.

*To whom God would make known what is the riches of the glory of this mystery among the Gentiles; which is **Christ in you**, the hope of glory.* Col. 1:27.

*There salute thee Epaphras, my fellowprisoner **in Christ Jesus**.* Phile. 23.

*And we know that the Son of God is come, and hath given us an understanding, that we may know him that is true, and we are **in him** that is true, even **in his Son Jesus Christ**. This is the true God, and eternal life.* I Jhn. 5:20.

*Jude, the servant of Jesus Christ, and brother of James, to them that are sanctified by God the Father, and preserved **in Jesus Christ**, and called.* Jude 1.

Again we ask, How can one be in Christ, if not in His Body?

7. The Church is *in* Christ.

It is because of the baptism of the Holy Ghost that the Church itself is said to be *in Christ*. This is a post Pentecost truth.

So we, <u>being many, are one body</u> in Christ, and every one member one of another. Rom. 12:5.

But of him are ye in Christ Jesus, who of God is made unto us wisdom, and righteousness, and sanctification, and redemption. I Cor. 1:30.

Now he which stablisheth us with you in Christ, and hath anointed us, is God. II Cor. 1:21.

And was unknown by face unto <u>the churches of Judaea</u> which were in Christ. Gal. 1:22.

There is neither Jew nor Greek, there is neither bond nor free, there is neither male nor female: for <u>ye are all one</u> in Christ Jesus. Gal. 3:28.

Paul and Timotheus, the servants of Jesus Christ, to <u>all the saints</u> in Christ Jesus which are at Philippi, with the bishops and deacons. Phil. 1:1.

To <u>the saints and faithful brethren</u> in Christ which are at Colosse: Grace be unto you, and peace, from God our Father and the Lord Jesus Christ. Col. 1:2.

Paul, and Silvanus, and Timotheus, unto the church of the Thessalonians which is in God the Father and in the Lord Jesus Christ. I Thess. 1:1.

For ye, brethren, became followers of <u>the churches of God which in Judaea</u> are in Christ Jesus. I Thess. 2:14.

45

Greet ye one another with a kiss of charity. Peace be with you all that are in Christ Jesus. Amen. I Pet. 5:14.

8. The Church fulfils the types of the Feast of Pentecost.

In the OT *Calendar of the Messiah* (See Lev. 23), Passover pointed to Christ's death, and the First Fruits of the Barley Harvest on the third day pointed to His resurrection. Therefore, fifty days later with the next feast, Pentecost, we would expect another major event to be foreshadowed and fulfilled. In the Firstfruits of the Barley Harvest after the Passover, an individual sheaf was waved before the Lord. At Pentecost, (First Fruits of the Wheat Harvest), the individual grains were baked into *loaves* (Lev. 23:17). Believers baptised by the Holy Spirit into a new body fulfil this type.

There were *two loaves*, pointing to the Jews being brought into the Body of Christ in Acts 2, and the Gentiles in Acts 10. See Acts 11:15-17. The fact that leaven was used in these loaves points to the Church's imperfect state. To say that the Church began with the calling of the disciples (Mk.3:13-19) would leave Pentecost alone among the seven OT feasts without a direct fulfilment.

15 And ye shall count unto you from the morrow after the sabbath, from the day that ye brought the sheaf of the wave offering; seven sabbaths shall be complete: 16 Even unto the morrow after the seventh sabbath shall ye number fifty days; and ye shall offer a new meat offering unto the LORD. 17 Ye shall bring out of your habitations two wave loaves of two tenth deals; they *shall be of fine flour; they shall be <u>baked with leaven</u>; they are the firstfruits unto the LORD. 18 And ye shall offer with the bread seven lambs without blemish of the first year, and one young bullock, and two rams: they shall be for a burnt offering unto the LORD, with their meat offering, and their drink offerings, even an offering made by fire, of sweet savor unto the LORD. 19 Then ye shall sacrifice one kid of the goats for a sin offering, and two lambs of the first year for a sacrifice of peace offerings. 20 And the priest shall <u>wave them</u> with the bread of the firstfruits for a wave offering before the LORD, with the two lambs: they shall be holy to the LORD for the priest.* Lev. 23:15-20.

9. The Church is the Temple of the Holy Spirit.

As such it could only be formed after Christ was glorified and the Holy Spirit poured out (Acts 2:33).

(But this spake he of the Spirit, which they that believe on him should receive: for <u>the Holy Ghost was not yet given; because that Jesus was not yet glorified</u>.) Jhn. 7:39.

Nevertheless I tell you the truth; It is expedient for you that I go away: for if I go not away, the Comforter will not come unto you; but if I depart, <u>I will send him unto you</u>. Jhn. 16:7.

Therefore <u>being by the right hand of God exalted</u>, and having received of the Father the promise of the Holy Ghost, <u>he hath shed forth this</u>, which ye now see and hear. Acts 2:33.

*Know ye not that ye are the **temple of God**, and that <u>the Spirit of God dwelleth in you</u>?* I Cor. 3:16.

*20 And are built upon the foundation of the apostles and prophets, Jesus Christ himself being **the chief corner stone**; 21 In whom all the **building** fitly framed together groweth unto an **holy temple** in the Lord: 22 In whom ye also are builded together for an **habitation of God through the Spirit**.* Eph. 2:20-22.

*But if I tarry long, that thou mayest know how thou oughtest to behave thyself in the **house of God**, which is the **church of the living God**, the pillar and ground of the truth.* I Tim. 3:15.

10. The Church is built upon the Apostles and Prophets.

In nine instances during our Lord's ministry the disciples were called apostles and were empowered by Him, but the actual gifts to fulfil that office came afterward. We do not see the disciples in the Gospels exercising the prophetic gift. Nor do we see them being a channel of the inspired Scriptures that were to come through them. Thus Ephesians speaks of Christ giving apostles and prophets *after* He ascended on high.

*Therefore also said the wisdom of God, I **will send them prophets and apostles**, and some of them they shall slay and persecute.* Lk. 11:49.

*Simon, Simon... **when thou art converted**, strengthen thy brethren.* Lk. 22:31,32.

48

*And **are built upon the foundation of the apostles and prophets**, Jesus Christ himself being the chief corner stone.* Eph. 2:20.

*8 Wherefore he saith, <u>When he ascended up on high</u>, he led captivity captive, and <u>gave gifts unto men</u>. 9 (Now that he ascended, what is it but that he also descended first into the lower parts of the earth? 10 He that descended is the same also that ascended up far above all heavens, that he might fill all things.) 11 And **he gave some, apostles; and some, prophets**; <u>and some, evangelists; and some, pastors and teachers</u>; 12 For the perfecting of the saints, for the work of the ministry, for the edifying of the <u>body of Christ</u>.* Eph. 4:8-12.

Simon Peter was hardly a foundation stone prior to the Day of Pentecost (at which time he faced 3000), for shortly before that day he could not face a single servant girl, (Mk. 14:66,67).

11. The Church is composed of Jew and Gentile.

The middle wall of partition was not broken down in the Gospel period, but rather *after* the Cross.

11 Wherefore remember, that <u>ye being in time past Gentiles</u> in the flesh, who are called Uncircumcision by that which is called the Circumcision in the flesh made by hands; 12 That at that time ye were without Christ, being <u>aliens from the commonwealth</u> of Israel, and strangers from the covenants of promise, having no hope, and without God in the world: 3 But now in Christ Jesus ye who sometimes were far off are <u>made nigh by the blood of Christ</u>. 14 For he is our peace, who hath <u>made both</u>

49

one, and hath broken down the middle wall of partition between us; 15 Having abolished in his flesh the enmity, even the law of commandments contained in ordinances; for to make in himself of twain one new man, so making peace; 16 And that he might reconcile both unto God in one body by the cross, having slain the enmity thereby. Eph. 2:11-16.

There is neither Jew nor Greek, there is neither bond nor free, there is neither male nor female: for ye are all one in Christ Jesus. Gal. 3:28.

That the Gentiles should be fellowheirs, and of the same body, and partakers of his promise in Christ by the gospel. Eph. 3:6.

Where there is neither Greek nor Jew, circumcision nor uncircumcision, Barbarian, Scythian, bond nor free: but Christ is all, and in all. Col. 3:11.

12. The Church is a Mystery.

Its first specific mention is near the end of Christ's earthly ministry, Mt. 16:18, and only revealed fully afterwards.

1 For this cause I Paul, the prisoner of Jesus Christ for you Gentiles, 2 If ye have heard of the dispensation of the grace of God which is given me to you-ward: 3 How that by revelation he made known unto me **the mystery**; *(as I wrote afore in few words, 4 Whereby, when ye read, ye may understand my knowledge in* **the mystery** *of Christ) 5 Which in other ages was not made known unto the sons of men, as it is now revealed unto his holy apostles and prophets by the Spirit; 6 That the Gentiles should be* *fellowheirs, and of the same body, and partakers of his promise in Christ by the gospel.* Eph. 3:1-6.

26 Even the mystery which hath been hid from ages and from generations, but now is made manifest to his saints: 27 To whom God would make known what is the riches of the glory of this mystery among the Gentiles; which is Christ in you, the hope of glory. Col. 1:26, 27.

13. The Church constitutes a new dispensation.

To place the church before the Cross, or to have it on both sides of the Cross confuses the dististinction between the dispensations of Law and Grace. To have a functioning Local Church under the dispensation of Law, *while* sacrifices where still being offered, *before* the Great Sacrifice, *before* the veil of the temple was rent, is unthinkable! The priesthood, ceremonies and offerings were the visible expression of the Dispensation of Law. The Local Church is the visible expression of the Dispensation of Grace.

For sin shall not have dominion over you: for ye are not under the law, but under grace. Rom. 6:14.

6 Who also hath made us able ministers of the new testament; not of the letter, but of the spirit: for the letter killeth, but the spirit giveth life. 7 But if the ministration of death, written and engraven in stones, was glorious, so that the children of Israel could not stedfastly behold the face of Moses for the glory of his countenance; which glory was to be done away: 8 How shall not the ministration of the spirit be rather glorious?

9 For if the <u>ministration of condemnation</u> be glory, much more doth the <u>ministration of righteousness</u> exceed in glory. II Cor. 6-9.

Christ hath <u>redeemed us from the curse of the law</u>, being made a curse for us: for it is written, Cursed is every one that hangeth on a tree. Gal. 3:13.

22 But the scripture hath concluded all under sin, that the promise by faith of Jesus Christ might be given to them that believe. 23 But before faith came, we were <u>kept under the law</u>, shut up unto the faith which should afterwards be revealed. 24 Wherefore <u>the law was our schoolmaster</u> to bring us unto Christ, that we might be justified by faith. 25 But after that faith is come, we are no longer under a schoolmaster. 26 For <u>ye are all the children of God</u> by faith in Christ Jesus. 27 For <u>as many of you as have been baptized into Christ have put on Christ</u>. Gal. 3:22-27.

4 But when the fulness of the time was come, God sent forth his Son, made of a woman, made under the law, 5 To redeem them that were under the law, that we might receive the adoption of sons. 6 And because ye are sons, God hath sent forth the Spirit of his Son into your hearts, crying, Abba, Father. 7 Wherefore thou art no more a servant, but a son; and if a son, then an heir of God through Christ. Gal. 4:4-7.

13 But now in Christ Jesus ye who sometimes were far off are <u>made nigh by the blood of Christ</u>. 14 For he is our peace, who hath <u>made both one, and hath broken down the middle wall of partition</u>

between us; 15 Having abolished in his flesh the enmity, even the law of commandments contained in ordinances; for to make in himself of twain one new man, so making peace; 16 And that he might reconcile both unto God in one body by the cross, having slain the enmity thereby. Eph. 2:13-16.

10 And ye are complete in him, which is the head of all principality and power: 11 In whom also ye are circumcised with the circumcision made without hands, in putting off the body of the sins of the flesh by the circumcision of Christ: 12 Buried with him in baptism, wherein also ye are risen with him through the faith of the operation of God, who hath raised him from the dead. 13 And you, being dead in your sins and the uncircumcision of your flesh, hath he quickened together with him, having forgiven you all trespasses; 14 Blotting out the handwriting of ordinances that was against us, which was contrary to us, and took it out of the way, nailing it to his cross. Col. 2:10-14.

Who gave himself for us, that he might redeem us from all iniquity, and purify unto himself a peculiar people, zealous of good works. Titus 2:14.

For the priesthood being changed, there is made of necessity a change also of the law. Heb. 7:12.

18 For there is verily a disannulling of the commandment going before for the weakness and unprofitableness thereof. 19 For the law made nothing perfect, but the bringing in of a better hope did; by the which we draw nigh unto God. Heb. 7:18-19.

In that he saith, A new covenant, he hath made the first old. Now that which decayeth and waxeth old is ready to vanish away. Heb. 8:13.

8 The Holy Ghost this signifying, that the way into the holiest of all was not yet made manifest, while as the first tabernacle was yet standing: 9 Which was a figure for the time then present, in which were offered both gifts and sacrifices, that could not make him that did the service perfect, as pertaining to the conscience; 10 Which stood only in meats and drinks, and divers washings, and carnal ordinances, imposed on them until the time of reformation. 11 But Christ being come an high priest of good things to come, by a greater and more perfect tabernacle, not made with hands, that is to say, not of this building; 12 Neither by the blood of goats and calves, but by his own blood he entered in once into the holy place, having obtained eternal redemption for us. 13 For if the blood of bulls and of goats, and the ashes of an heifer sprinkling the unclean, sanctifieth to the purifying of the flesh: 14 How much more shall the blood of Christ, who through the eternal Spirit offered himself without spot to God, purge your conscience from dead works to serve the living God? 15 And for this cause he is the mediator of the new testament, that by means of death, for the redemption of the transgressions that were under the first testament, they which are called might receive the promise of eternal inheritance. 16 For where a testament is, there must also of necessity be the death of the testator. 17 For a testament is of force after men are dead: otherwise it

54

is of no strength at all while the testator liveth. Heb. 9:8-17.

For the law having a shadow of good things to come, and not the very image of the things, can never with those sacrifices which they offered year by year continually make the comers thereunto perfect. Heb. 10:1.

9 Then said he, Lo, I come to do thy will, O God. He taketh away the first, that he may establish the second. 10 By the which will we are sanctified through the offering of the body of Jesus Christ once for all. Heb. 10:9,10.

18 Now where remission of these is, there is no more offering for sin. 19 Having therefore, brethren, boldness to enter into the holiest by the blood of Jesus, 20 By a new and living way, which he hath consecrated for us, through the veil, that is to say, his flesh; 21 And having an high priest over the house of God; 22 Let us draw near with a true heart in full assurance of faith, having our hearts sprinkled from an evil conscience, and our bodies washed with pure water. 23 Let us hold fast the profession of our faith without wavering; (for he is faithful that promised;) 24 And let us consider one another to provoke unto love and to good works: 25 Not forsaking the assembling of ourselves together, as the manner of some is; but exhorting one another: and so much the more, as ye see the day approaching. Heb. 10:18-25.

14. A Kingdom rather than a Local Church message was proclaimed during the ministries of Christ and John the Baptist.

A chapter-by-chapter survey will show the kingdom emphasis in the Gospels, and that to the Jews. There is no indication of believers being instructed to become part of a Local Church.

*1 In those days came John the Baptist, preaching in the wilderness of Judaea, 2 And saying, Repent ye: for **the kingdom of heaven** is at hand. 3 For this is he that was spoken of by the prophet Esaias, saying, The voice of one crying in the wilderness, Prepare ye the way of the Lord, make his paths straight.* Mt. 3:1-3.

*17 From that time Jesus began to preach, and to say, Repent: for **the kingdom of heaven** is at hand. 18 And Jesus, walking by the sea of Galilee, saw two brethren, Simon called Peter, and Andrew his brother, casting a net into the sea: for they were fishers. 19 And he saith unto them, Follow me, and I will make you fishers of men. 20 And they straightway left their nets, and followed him.* Mt. 4:17-20.

*1 And seeing the multitudes, he went up into a mountain: and when he was set, his disciples came unto him: 2 And he opened his mouth, and taught them, saying, 3 Blessed are the poor in spirit: for theirs is **the kingdom of heaven**.* Mt. 5:1-3.

*But seek ye first **the kingdom of God**, and his righteousness; and all these things shall be added unto you.* Mt. 6:33.

*Not every one that saith unto me, Lord, Lord, shall enter into **the kingdom of heaven**; but he that doeth the will of my Father which is in heaven.* Mt. 7:21.

*And Jesus went about all the cities and villages, teaching in their synagogues, and preaching **the gospel of the kingdom**, and healing every sickness and every disease among the people.* Mt. 9:35.

*5 These twelve Jesus sent forth, and commanded them, saying, <u>Go not into the way of the Gentiles</u>, and into any city of the Samaritans enter ye not: 6 But <u>go rather to the lost sheep of the house of Israel</u>. 7 And as ye go, preach, saying, **The kingdom of heaven** <u>is at hand</u>.* Mt. 10:5-7.

*11 Verily I say unto you, Among them that are born of women there hath not risen a greater than John the Baptist: notwithstanding he that is least in **the kingdom of heaven** is greater than he. 12 And from the days of John the Baptist until now **the kingdom of heaven** <u>suffereth violence</u>, and the violent take it by force. 13 For all the prophets and the law prophesied until John. 14 And <u>if ye will receive it, this is Elias</u>, which was for to come.* Mt. 11:11-14.

*But if I cast out devils by the Spirit of God, then **the kingdom of God** <u>is come unto you</u>.* Mt. 12:28.

1 The same day went Jesus out of the house, and sat by the sea side. 2 And great multitudes were gathered together unto him, so that he went into a *ship, and sat; and the whole multitude stood on the shore. 3 And he spake many things unto them in parables, saying, Behold, a sower went forth to sow; 10 And the disciples came, and said unto him, Why speakest thou unto them in parables? 11 He answered and said unto them, Because it is given unto you to know **the mysteries of the kingdom of heaven**, but to them it is not given.* Mt. 13:1-3,10,11.

*19 And I will give unto thee **the keys of the kingdom of heaven**: and whatsoever thou shalt bind on earth shall be bound in heaven: and whatsoever thou shalt loose on earth shall be loosed in heaven. 20 Then charged he his disciples that they should tell no man that he was Jesus the Christ. 21 From that time forth began Jesus to shew unto his disciples, how that he must go unto Jerusalem, and suffer many things of the elders and chief priests and scribes, and be killed, and be raised again the third day.* Mt. 16:19-21.

*Verily I say unto you, There be some standing here, which shall not taste of death, till they see the Son of man coming in **his kingdom**.* Mt. 16:28.

*1 At the same time came the disciples unto Jesus, saying, Who is the greatest in **the kingdom of heaven**? 2 And Jesus called a little child unto him, and set him in the midst of them, 3 And said, Verily I say unto you, Except ye be converted, and become as little children, ye shall not enter into **the kingdom of heaven**. 4 Whosoever therefore shall humble himself as this little child, the same is greatest in **the kingdom of heaven**.* Mt. 18:1-4.

*Therefore is **the kingdom of heaven** likened unto a certain king, which would take account of his servants.* Mt. 18:23.

*But Jesus said, Suffer little children, and forbid them not, to come unto me: for of such is **the kingdom of heaven**.* Mt. 19:14.

*23 Then said Jesus unto his disciples, Verily I say unto you, That a rich man shall hardly enter into **the kingdom of heaven**. 24 And again I say unto you, It is easier for a camel to go through the eye of a needle, than for a rich man to enter into **the kingdom of God**.* Mt. 19:23,24.

*For **the kingdom of heaven** is like unto a man that is an householder, which went out early in the morning to hire labourers into his vineyard.* Mt. 20:1

*Whether of them twain did the will of his father? They say unto him, The first. Jesus saith unto them, Verily I say unto you, That <u>the publicans and the harlots go into</u> **the kingdom of God** before you.* Mt. 21:31.

*Therefore say I unto you, **The kingdom of God** <u>shall be taken from you</u>, and given to a nation bringing forth the fruits thereof.* Mt. 21:43.

***The kingdom of heaven** is like unto a certain king, which made a marriage for his son.* Mt. 22:2.

*But woe unto you, scribes and Pharisees, hypocrites! for <u>ye shut up</u> **the kingdom of heaven** against men: for ye neither go in yourselves, neither suffer ye them that are entering to go in.* Mt. 23:13.

*Then shall **the kingdom of heaven** be likened unto ten virgins, which took their lamps, and went forth to meet the bridegroom. Mt. 25:1.*

*For **the kingdom of heaven** is as a man travelling into a far country, who called his own servants, and delivered unto them his goods. Mt. 25:14.*

*Then shall the King say unto them on his right hand, Come, ye blessed of my Father, inherit **the kingdom** prepared for you from the foundation of the world. Mt. 25:34.*

*But I say unto you, I will not drink henceforth of this fruit of the vine, until that day when I drink it new with you in **my Father's kingdom**. Mt. 26:29.*

This same Kingdom emphasis is seen in Mark and Luke. Again, there is no mention or indication that those who responded to Christ, John the Baptist and the disciples were to be joined to a church. Note several passages:

*14 Now after that John was put in prison, Jesus came into Galilee, preaching the gospel of **the kingdom of God**, 15 And saying, The time is fulfilled, and **the kingdom of God** is at hand: repent ye, and believe the gospel. Mk. 1:14,15.*

*And he said unto them, I must preach **the kingdom of God** to other cities also: for therefore am I sent. Lk. 4:43.*

And it came to pass afterward, that he went throughout every city and village, preaching and shewing the glad tidings of **the kingdom of God***: and the twelve were with him.* Lk. 8:1.

1 Then he called his twelve disciples together, and gave them power and authority over all devils, and to cure diseases. 2 And he sent them to preach **the kingdom of God***, and to heal the sick.* Lk. 9:1,2.

And the people, when they knew it, followed him: and he received them, and spake unto them of **the kingdom of God***, and healed them that had need of healing.* Lk. 9:11.

60 Jesus said unto him, Let the dead bury their dead: but go thou and preach **the kingdom of God***. 61 And another also said, Lord, I will follow thee; but let me first go bid them farewell, which are at home at my house. 62 And Jesus said unto him, No man, having put his hand to the plough, and looking back, is fit for* **the kingdom of God***.* Lk. 9:60-62.

9 And heal the sick that are therein, and say unto them, **The kingdom of God** *is come nigh unto you. 10 But into whatsoever city ye enter, and they receive you not, go your ways out into the streets of the same, and say, 11 Even the very dust of your city, which cleaveth on us, we do wipe off against you: notwithstanding be ye sure of this, that* **the kingdom of God** *is come nigh unto you.* Lk. 10:9-11.

Dispensationalists rightly understand that this message referred to the same literal Kingdom that was emphasised in Isaiah to Malachi. When we go from Malachi to Matthew there is no difference in the kind of Kingdom being offered. The Jews rejection of this Kingdom was the means by which the Father offered up

His Son as *the Lamb of God, which taketh away the sin of the world* (Jhn. 1:29).

The kingdom is mentioned three times in the Gospel of John (3:3,5; 18:36). It is to be stressed that this Gospel gives no mention or indication of a Local Church. Not in our Lord's dealings with individuals: Nicodemus, the woman at the well, the nobleman, the lame man at the pool, the woman taken in adultery, the man born blind, Mary, Martha, Lazarus. Nor in dealings with multitudes: the five thousand and other large gatherings. If Christ with His disciples constituted a Local Church, why do we not read of these multitudes and individuals being added to it?

After Christ's resurrection, it was the kingdom that still occupied the apostles thinking.

> *When they therefore were come together, they asked of him, saying, Lord, wilt thou at this time restore again **the kingdom** to Israel?* Acts 1:6.

15. Before the Cross, there is no stated connection between Baptism and a supposed already existing Local Church.

There is no indication that believers in that period were added to or became a part of a Local Church through baptism. If the Local Church was present, why is this not so expressed?

> *6 And were **baptized** of him in Jordan, confessing their sins. 7 But when he saw many of the Pharisees and Sadducees come to **his baptism**, he said unto them, O generation of vipers, who hath warned you to flee from the wrath to come? 8 Bring forth therefore fruits meet for repentance: 9 And think not to say within yourselves, We have Abraham*

62

to our father: for I say unto you, that God is able of these stones to raise up children unto Abraham. 10 And now also the axe is laid unto the root of the trees: therefore every tree which bringeth not forth good fruit is hewn down, and cast into the fire. 11 I indeed **baptize you with water** <u>unto repentance</u>*: but he that cometh after me is mightier than I, whose shoes I am not worthy to bear: he shall baptize you with the Holy Ghost, and with fire.* Mt. 3:6-11.

The baptism of John, *whence was it? from heaven, or of men? And they reasoned with themselves, saying, If we shall say, From heaven; he will say unto us, Why did ye not then believe him?* Mt. 21:25.

4 John did **baptize** *in the wilderness, and preach* **the baptism** <u>of repentance</u> *for the remission of   sins. 5 And there went out unto him all the land of Judaea, and they of Jerusalem, and were all* **baptized** *of him in the river of Jordan,* <u>confessing their sins</u>. Mk. 1:4,5.

7 Then said he to the multitude that came forth to be **baptized** *of him, O generation of vipers, who hath warned you to flee from the wrath to come? 8 Bring forth therefore* <u>fruits worthy of repentance</u>*, and begin not to say within yourselves, We have Abraham to our father: for I say unto you, That God is able of these stones to raise up children unto Abraham. 9 And now also the axe is laid unto the root of the trees: every tree therefore which bringeth not forth good fruit is hewn down, and cast into the fire. 10 And the people asked him, saying,*

What shall we do then? 11 He answereth and saith unto them, He that hath two coats, let him impart to him that hath none; and he that hath meat, let him do likewise. 12 Then came also publicans to be **baptized***, and said unto him, Master, who shall we do? 13 And he said unto them, Exact no more than that which is appointed you. 14 And the soldiers likewise demanded of him, saying, And who shall we do? And he said unto them, Do violence to no man, neither accuse any falsely; and be content with your wages.* Lk. 3:7-14.

Now when all the people were **baptized***, it came to pass, that Jesus also being* **baptized***, and praying, the heaven was opened.* Lk. 3:21.

29 And all the people that heard him, and the publicans, justified God, being **baptized with the baptism of John***. 30 But the Pharisees and lawyers rejected the counsel of God against themselves, being not* **baptized** *of him.* Lk. 7:29,30.

And I knew him not: but he that sent me to **baptize with water***, the same said unto me, Upon whom thou shalt see the Spirit descending, and remaining on him, the same is he which baptizeth with the Holy Ghost.* Jhn. 1:33.

22 After these things came Jesus and his disciples into the land of Judaea; and there he tarried with them, and **baptized***. 23 And John also was* **baptizing** *in Aenon near to Salim, because there was* much water there*: and they came, and were* **baptized***. 24 For John was not yet cast into prison. 25 Then there arose a question between some of John's disciples and the Jews about purifying. 26*

*And they came unto John, and said unto him, Rabbi, he that was with thee beyond Jordan, to whom thou barest witness, behold, the same **baptizeth**, and all men come to him. 27 John answered and said, A man can receive nothing, except it be given him from heaven.* Jhn. 3:22-27.

*24 And a certain Jew named Apollos, born at Alexandria, an eloquent man, and mighty in the scriptures, came to Ephesus. 25 This man was instructed in the way of the Lord; and being fervent in the spirit, he spake and taught diligently the things of the Lord, knowing only **the baptism of John**. 26 And he began to speak boldly in the synagogue: whom when Aquila and Priscilla had heard, they took him unto them, and expounded unto him the way of God more perfectly.* Acts 18:24-25.

*1 And it came to pass, that, while Apollos was at Corinth, Paul having passed through the upper coasts came to Ephesus: and finding certain disciples, 2 He said unto them, Have ye received the Holy Ghost since ye believed? And they said unto him, We have not so much as heard whether there be any Holy Ghost. 3 And he said unto them, Unto what then were ye **baptized**? And they said, Unto **John's baptism**. 4 Then said Paul, John verily baptized with **the baptism** <u>of repentance</u>, saying unto the people, that <u>they should believe on him which should come after him</u>, that is, on Christ Jesus. 5 When they heard this, they were **baptized** in the name of the Lord Jesus. 6 And when Paul had laid his hands upon them, the Holy Ghost came on them; and they spake with tongues, and prophesied.* Acts 19:1-6.

16. Pentecost is specifically called a "beginning" in Acts 11:15.

A beginning, of course says that something is now starting. What is this beginning? What is now starting? If not the Church, then what?

*And as I began to speak, the Holy Ghost fell on them, as on us **at the beginning**.*

CHAPTER 3

Post Pentecost Names Given to the Church

The idea that the Church began with the calling of the disciples is the primary plank of Landmarkism. An obvious argument against this, is that the names given to the Church are all *post* and not *pre* Pentecost. Indeed, as we have seen, the word "Church" itself is not used of an assembled gathering until after Pentecost (Acts 2:47). Nor were those assembled in the upper room in Acts 1, shortly before Pentecost, called a Church. This same is true of eight other names.

While in a great majority of instances these names are applied to the Local Church, there are clear instances where an *unforced* reading requires that they must refer to the redeemed generally. That believers are to fellowship and serve in a Local Church is the great emphasis of the New Testament. Christ rather than hierarchal structures is its Head. In a tangible and visible sense the Local Church is the Body, Building, House, Temple, Assembly, Gathering, Priesthood, and perhaps Bride of Christ. It soon becomes apparent, however, that there are instances where these terms go beyond the local assembly. The Bible believer should be able to see this.

1. The Church.

Nearly every time the word "Church" is found in the New Testament it is the Local Church. The very meaning and usage of the word is that of believers who are *called out* to *assemble*. Therefore the term "universal church" is a misnomer, and an incorrect concept. It gives a wrong impression, and is not a term that Independent

Baptists generally use. The term "universal church" places the emphasis upon *horizontal* unity between churches, and has been a basis for ecumenism. The view we hold to be Scriptural, places the emphasis upon our *vertical* union with Christ and then fellowship with other churches, as is possible, and within clearly marked Biblical bounds.

In my daily tract distribution work on the streets of London, I meet some (not many over here!) who are clearly saved, clearly joined to Christ, and we can have a good warm conversation. But it soon becomes apparent, that any thing approaching Local Church fellowship will probably have to wait till we get to Heaven. We are both joined to Christ, we are both in Local Churches, but there is nothing very "universal" about it. The vertical is there, but not the horizontal.

A number of passages speak of the Church in a more singular, collective or generic sense.

> *And I say also unto thee, That thou art Peter, and upon this rock I will build **my church**; and the gates of hell shall not prevail against it.* Mt. 16:18.

> *As for Saul, he made havock of the **church**, <u>entering into every house</u>, and haling men and women committed them to prison.* Acts 8:3.

> *Take heed therefore unto yourselves, and to <u>all the flock</u>, over the which the Holy Ghost hath made you overseers, to feed **the church of God**, which he hath purchased with his own blood.* Acts 20:28.

> *Give none offence, neither to the Jews, nor to the Gentiles, nor to **the church of God**.* I Cor. 10:32.

*For I am the least of the apostles, that am not meet to be called an apostle, because I persecuted **the church of God**.* I Cor. 15:9.

*For ye have heard of my conversation in time past in the Jews' religion, how that beyond measure I persecuted **the church of God**, and wasted it.* Gal. 1:13.

*And hath put all things under his feet, and gave him to be <u>the head</u> over all things to **the church**.* Eph. 1:22.

*To the intent that now unto the principalities and powers in heavenly places might be known by **the church** the manifold wisdom of God.* Eph. 3:10.

*Unto him be glory in **the church** by Christ Jesus throughout all ages, world without end. Amen.* Eph. 3:21.

*22 Wives, submit yourselves unto your own husbands, as unto the Lord. 23 For the husband is the head of the wife, even as Christ is the head of **the church**: and he is the saviour of <u>the body</u>. 24 Therefore as **the church** is subject unto Christ, so let the wives be to their own husbands in every thing. 25 Husbands, love your wives, even as Christ also loved **the church**, and gave himself for it; 26 That he might sanctify and cleanse it with the washing of water by the word, 27 That he might present it to himself **a glorious church**, not having spot, or wrinkle, or any such thing; but that it should be holy and without blemish. 28 So ought men to love their wives as their own bodies. He that loveth his wife loveth himself. 29 For no man ever yet hated his own flesh; but* *nourisheth and cherisheth it, even as the Lord* **the church***: 30 For we are* <u>members of his body, of his flesh, and of his bones</u>*. 31 For this cause shall a man leave his father and mother, and shall be joined unto his wife, and they two shall be one flesh. 32 This is* <u>a great mystery</u>*: but I speak concerning Christ and* **the church***.* Eph. 5:22-32.

And he is the <u>head of the body</u>*,* **the church***: who is the beginning, the firstborn from the dead; that in all things he might have the preeminence.* Col. 1:18.

Who now rejoice in my sufferings for you, and fill up that which is behind of the afflictions of Christ in my flesh for <u>his body's sake</u>*, which is* **the church***.* Col. 1:24.

But if I tarry long, that thou mayest know how thou oughtest to behave thyself in <u>the house of God</u>*, which is* **the church of the living God***,* <u>the pillar and ground</u> *of the truth.* I Tim. 3:15.

Saying, I will declare thy name unto my brethren, in the midst of **the church** *will I sing praise unto thee.* Heb. 2:12.

To the <u>general assembly</u> *and* **church of the firstborn***, which are written in heaven, and to God the Judge of all, and to the spirits of just men made perfect.* Heb. 12:23.

2. The Body

4 For as we have many members in **one body***, and all members have not the same office: 5 So we,* *being many, are **one body in Christ**, and every one members one of another.* Rom. 12:4,5.

*For we being many are <u>one bread</u>, and **one body**: for we are all partakers of that one bread.* I Cor. 10:17.

*12 For as <u>the body is one</u>, and hath many members, and all the members of that **one body**, being many, are **one body**: so also is Christ. 13 For by one Spirit are we all baptized into **one body**, whether we be Jews or Gentiles, whether we be bond or free; and have been all made to drink into one Spirit. 14 For the body is not one member, but many. 15 If the foot shall say, Because I am not the hand, I am not of the body; is it therefore not of the body? 16 And if the ear shall say, Because I am not the eye, I am not of the body; is it therefore not of the body? 17 If the whole body were an eye, where were the hearing? If the whole were hearing, where were the smelling? 18 But now hath God set the members every one of them in **the body**, as it hath pleased him. 19 And if they were all one member, where were **the body**? 20 But now are they many members, yet but **one body**. 21 And the eye cannot say unto the hand, I have no need of thee: nor again the head to the feet, I have no need of you. 22 Nay, much more those members of **the body**, which seem to be more feeble, are necessary: 23 And those members of **the body**, which we think to be less honourable, upon these we bestow more abundant honour; and our uncomely parts have more abundant comeliness. 24 For our comely parts have no need: but God hath tempered **the body** together, having given more abundant* *honour to that part which lacked. 25 That there should be no schism in **the body**; but that the members should have the same care one for another. 26 And whether one member suffer, all the members suffer with it; or one member be honoured, all the members rejoice with it. 27 Now ye are **the body of Christ**, and members in particular.* I Cor. 12:12-27.

*22 And hath put all things under his feet, and gave him to be the <u>head over all things to the church</u>, 23 Which is **his body**, the fulness of him that filleth all in all.* Eph. 1:22,23.

*And that he might reconcile both unto God in **one body** by the cross, having slain the enmity thereby.* Eph. 2:16.

*That the Gentiles should be fellowheirs, and of **the same body**, and partakers of his promise in Christ by the gospel.* Eph. 3:6.

*There is **one body**, and <u>one Spirit</u>, even as ye are called in <u>one hope</u> of your calling.* Eph. 4:4.

*11 And he gave some, apostles; and some, prophets; and some, evangelists; and some, pastors and teachers; 12 For the perfecting of the saints, for the work of the ministry, for the edifying of **the body of Christ**.* Eph. 4:11,12.

*From whom **the whole body** fitly joined together and compacted by that which every joint supplieth, according to the effectual working in the measure of every part, maketh increase of **the body** unto the edifying of itself in love.* Eph. 4:16.

*For the husband is the head of the wife, even as Christ is the <u>head of the church</u>: and he is the <u>saviour of</u> **the body**.* Eph. 5:23.

*For we are members of **his body**, of his flesh, and of his bones.* Eph. 5:30.

*And he is the <u>head of</u> **the body**, <u>the church</u>: who is the beginning, the firstborn from the dead; that in all things he might have the preeminence.* Col. 1:18.

*Who now rejoice in my sufferings for you, and fill up that which is behind of the afflictions of Christ in my flesh for **his body's sake**, which is <u>the church</u>.* Col. 1:24.

*And not holding the Head, from which all the **body** by joints and bands having nourishment ministered, and knit together, increaseth with the increase of God.* Col. 2:19.

*And let the peace of God rule in your hearts, to the which also ye are called in **one body**; and be ye thankful.* Col. 3:15.

3. A Building

*For we are labourers together with God: ye are <u>God's husbandry</u>, ye are **God's building**.* I Cor. 3:9.

*In whom all the **building** fitly framed together groweth unto <u>an holy temple</u> in the Lord.* Eph. 2:21.

4 <u>To whom coming, as unto a living stone</u>, disallowed indeed of men, but chosen of God, and precious, 5 <u>Ye also, as lively stones, are built up a spiritual house</u>, an holy priesthood, to offer up *spiritual sacrifices, acceptable to God by Jesus Christ. 6 Wherefore also it is contained in the scripture, Behold, <u>I lay in Sion a chief corner stone</u>, elect, precious: and he that believeth on him shall not be confounded. 7 Unto you therefore which believe he is precious: but unto them which be disobedient, <u>the stone</u> which the builders disallowed, the same is made <u>the head of the corner,</u> 8 And a stone of stumbling, and a rock of offence, even to them which stumble at the word, being disobedient: whereunto also they were appointed. 9 But ye are a <u>chosen generation</u>, a <u>royal priesthood</u>, an <u>holy nation</u>, a <u>peculiar people</u>; that ye should shew forth the praises of him who hath called you out of darkness into his marvellous light.* I Pet. 2:4-9.

4. A House

As we have therefore opportunity, let us do good unto all men, especially unto them who are of **the household of faith**. Gal. 6:10.

Now therefore ye are no more strangers and foreigners, but <u>fellowcitizens</u> with the saints, and of **the household of God**. Eph. 2:19.

But if I tarry long, that thou mayest know how thou oughtest to behave thyself in **the house of God**, *which is <u>the church of the living God</u>, <u>the pillar and ground</u> of the truth.* I Tim. 3:15.

But in **a great house** *there are not only vessels of gold and of silver, but also of wood and of earth; and some to honour, and some to dishonour.* II Tim. 2:20.

74

*2 Who was faithful to him that appointed him, as also Moses was faithful in all <u>his house</u>. 3 For this man was counted worthy of more glory than Moses, inasmuch as he who hath builded **the house** hath more honour than **the house**. 4 For every house is builded by some man; but he that built all things is God. 5 And Moses verily was faithful in all <u>his house</u>, as a servant, for a testimony of those things which were to be spoken after; 6 But Christ as a son over **his own house**; whose **house** are we, if we hold fast the confidence and the rejoicing of the hope firm unto the end.* Heb. 3:2-6.

*And having an high priest over **the house of God**.* Heb. 10:21.

*5 Ye also, as lively stones, are built up **a spiritual house**, <u>an holy priesthood</u>, to offer up spiritual sacrifices, acceptable to God by Jesus Christ. 6 Wherefore also it is contained in the scripture, Behold, I lay in Sion a <u>chief corner stone</u>, elect, precious: and he that believeth on him shall not be confounded. 7 Unto you therefore which believe he is precious: but unto them which be disobedient, the stone which the builders disallowed, the same is made <u>the head of the corner</u>.* I Pet. 2:5-7.

*For the time is come that judgment must begin at **the house of God**: and if it first begin at us, what shall the end be of them that obey not the gospel of God?* I Pet. 4:17.

5. A Temple

*16 Know ye not that ye are **the temple of God**, and that the Spirit of God dwelleth in you?*

*17 If any man defile **the temple of God**, him shall God destroy; for **the temple of God** is holy, which **temple** ye are. I Cor. 3:16,17.*

*And what agreement hath **the temple of God** with idols? for ye are **the temple of the living God**; as God hath said, I will dwell in them, and walk in them; and I will be their God, and they shall be my people. II Cor. 6:16.*

*In whom <u>all the building</u> fitly framed together groweth unto **an holy temple** in the Lord. Eph. 2:21.*

6. An Assembly

*To **the general assembly** and <u>church of the firstborn</u>, which are written in heaven, and to God the Judge of all, and to the spirits of just men made perfect. Heb. 12:23.*

*For if there come unto **your assembly** a man with a gold ring, in goodly apparel, and there come in also a poor man in vile raiment; James 2:2.*

7. A Gathering.

A comparison of each of the times the word is used will demonstrate the difference in gatherings before and after Pentecost. The former is clearly not a church, the latter is.

*And **great multitudes were gathered together unto him**, so that he went into a ship, and sat; and the whole multitude stood on the shore. Mt. 13:32.*

19 Again I say unto you, That if two of you <u>shall</u> agree on earth as touching any thing that they <u>shall</u> ask, it <u>shall</u> be done for them of my Father *which is in heaven. 20 For **where two or three are gathered together in my name**, there am I in the midst of them.* Mt. 18:19,20.

*And **the apostles gathered themselves together unto Jesus**, and told him all things, both what they had done, and what they had taught.* Mk. 6:30.

*And when **much people were gathered together**, and were come to him out of every city, he spake by a parable.* Lk. 8:4.

*And when **the people were gathered thick together**, he began to say, This is an evil generation: they seek a sign; and there shall no sign be given it, but the sign of Jonas the prophet.* Lk. 11:29.

*In the mean time, when there **were gathered together an innumerable multitude** of people, insomuch that they trode one upon another, he began to say unto his disciples first of all, Beware ye of the leaven of the Pharisees, which is hypocrisy.* Lk. 12:1.

*And not for that nation only, but that also **he should gather together in one the children of God** that were scattered abroad.* Jhn. 11:52.

*And when he had considered the thing, he came to the house of Mary the mother of John, whose surname was Mark; where **many were gathered together praying**.* Acts 12:12.

*And when they were come, and had **gathered the church together**, they rehearsed all that God had done with them, and how he had opened the door of faith unto the Gentiles.* Acts 14:27.

*So when they were dismissed, they came to Antioch: and when they had **gathered the multitude together**, they delivered the epistle.* Acts 15:30.

*And there were many lights in the upper chamber, **where they were gathered together.*** Acts 20:8.

*In the name of our Lord Jesus Christ, **when ye are gathered together**, and my spirit, with the power of our Lord Jesus Christ.* I Cor. 5:4.

*That in the dispensation of the fulness of times **he might gather together in one all things in Christ, both which are in heaven, and which are on earth;** even in him.* Eph. 1:10.

*Now we beseech you, brethren, by the coming of our Lord Jesus Christ, and by **our gathering together unto him**.* II Thess. 2:1.

8. A Priesthood

I beseech you therefore, brethren, by the mercies of God, that ye present your bodies a living sacrifice, holy, acceptable unto God, which is your reasonable service. Rom. 12:1.

But I have all, and abound: I am full, having received of Epaphroditus the things which were sent from you, an odour of a sweet smell, a sacrifice acceptable, wellpleasing to God. Phil. 4:18.

By him therefore let us offer the sacrifice of praise to God continually, that is, the fruit of our lips giving thanks to his name. But to do good and to communicate forget not: for with such sacrifices God is well pleased. Heb. 13:15,16.

*Ye also, as <u>lively stones</u>, are built up <u>a spiritual house</u>, **an holy priesthood**, to offer up <u>spiritual sacrifices</u>, acceptable to God by Jesus Christ.* I Pet. 2: 5.

*But ye are <u>a chosen generation</u>, **a royal priesthood**, <u>an holy nation</u>, <u>a peculiar people</u>; that ye should shew forth the praises of him who hath called you out of darkness into his marvellous light.* I Pet. 2:9.

*And hath made us <u>kings</u> and **priests** unto God and his Father; to him be glory and dominion for ever and ever. Amen.* Rev. 1:6.

*And hast made us unto our God <u>kings</u> and **priests**: and we shall reign on the earth.* Rev. 5:10.

*Blessed and holy is he that hath part in the first resurrection: on such the second death hath no power, but they shall be **priests** of God and of Christ, and shall reign with him a thousand years.* Rev. 20:6.

9. A Bride, Virgin, Wife

19 And Jesus said unto them, Can the <u>children of the bridechamber</u> fast, while <u>the bridegroom</u> is with them? as long as they have <u>the bridegroom</u> with them, they cannot fast. 20 But the days will come, when <u>the bridegroom</u> shall be taken away from them, and then shall they fast in those days. Mk. 2:19-20.

*28 Ye yourselves bear me witness, that I said, I am not the Christ, but that I am sent before him. 29 He that hath **the bride** is <u>the bridegroom</u>: but the <u>friend of the bridegroom</u>, which standeth and* *heareth him, rejoiceth greatly because of <u>the bridegroom's voice</u>: this my joy therefore is fulfilled.* Jhn. 3:28-29.

*For I am jealous over you with godly jealousy: for I have espoused you to <u>one husband</u>, that I may present you as **a chaste virgin to Christ**.* II Cor. 11:2.

23 For the husband is the head of the wife, even as Christ is the <u>head of the church</u>: and he is the <u>saviour of the body</u>. 24 Therefore <u>as the church is subject unto Christ</u>, so let the wives be to their own husbands in every thing. 25 Husbands, love your wives, even as <u>Christ also loved the church</u>, and <u>gave himself for it;</u> 26 That he might sanctify and cleanse it with the washing of water by the word, 27 That he might <u>present it to himself a glorious church, not having spot, or wrinkle</u>, or any such thing; but that it should be holy and without blemish. 28 So ought men to love their wives as their own bodies. He that loveth his wife loveth himself. 29 For no man ever yet hated his own flesh; but nourisheth and cherisheth it, even <u>as the Lord the church</u>: 30 For <u>we are members of his body, of his flesh, and of his bones</u>. 31 For this cause shall a man leave his father and mother, and shall be joined unto his wife, and they two shall be one flesh. 32 <u>This is a great mystery: but I speak concerning Christ and the church</u>. Eph. 5:23-32.

*And I John saw the holy city, new Jerusalem, coming down from God out of heaven, prepared as **a bride** adorned for her husband.* Rev. 21:2.

*And there came unto me one of the seven angels which had the seven vials full of the seven last plagues, and talked with me, saying, Come hither, I will shew thee **the bride, the Lamb's wife**.* Rev. 21:9.

*And the Spirit and **the bride** say, Come. And let him that heareth say, Come. And let him that is athirst come. And whosoever will, let him take the water of life freely.* Rev. 22:17.

Conclusion

Under the heading "Four Reasons Why the Church Began at Pentecost" Lewis Sperry Chafer in his *Systematic Theology* writes the following:

a. There could be no Church in the world - constituted as she is and distinctive in all her features - until Christ's death; for her relation to that death is not a mere anticipation, but is based wholly on His finished work and she must be purified by His precious blood.

b. There could be no Church until Christ arose from the dead to provide her with resurrection life.

c. There could be no Church until He had ascended up on high to become her Head; for she is a New Creation with a new federal headship in the resurrected Christ. He is, likewise, to her as the head is to the body. Nor could the Church survive for a moment were it not for His intercession and advocacy in heaven.

d. There could be no Church on earth until the advent of the Holy Spirit; for the most basic and fundamental reality respecting the Church is that she is a temple for the habitation of God through the Spirit. She is regenerated, baptized, and sealed by the Spirit.

If it be contended that these conditions could have existed before Pentecost, it is easily proved that the Scriptures do not declare that these relationships were obtained until *after* Pentecost (cf. John 14:17). A Church without the finished work on which to stand; a Church without resurrection position or life; a Church which is a new humanity, but lacking a federal head; and a Church without Pentecost and all that Pentecost contributes, is only a figment of theological fancy and wholly extraneous to the New Testament. (vol. iv; pp. 45,46).

The *Revised Landmarkism* presented in this paper is not a friend to Independent Baptists. It is a forced, superimposed interpretation. It is divisive and becomes an obsession. It is contradictory, and incapable of reasonable defence. It has tenets, which seem to undermine the believer's position in Christ.

Along these lines, the *EBTS Journal* (Fall/Winter 2006) was an eye opener. Nearly a hundred pages were given to two articles: *Seven Fatal Flaws of Fundamentalism* by Ken Brooks, and *A Critique of Historical Fundamentalism* by Dr. W. Aaron Strouse. Both attack the fundamentalism that arose in America in the late 19th and early 20th Centuries. Their chief criticism was the movement's lack of emphasis on the Local Church, acceptance of a universal Church, interdenominationalism, no clarity on the mode of baptism, fundamentalism's acceptance of the critical text etc. And to this we say, Amen! These are justifiable points of criticism that must be addressed by every fundamentalist. However, the authors go too far.

What the authors fail to point out is that many in that time, while recognizing that we are joined to the spiritual Body of Christ at conversion, *did* take a strong Local Church stand and *did* teach Baptist distinctives. But, it is primarily because fundamentalism did/does not believe the kind of *revised Landmarkism* EBTS espouses

84

that the entire movement must be rejected. Due to this one singular aspect the movement is so flawed that the only solution is to *flee from it* (page 117). Reading these articles, you would be pressed to find a modernist or new evangelical with harder things to say about fundamentalism. The two authors have somehow succeeded in blaming the movement for just about every ill Independent Baptists face today.

The authors fail to mention that in addition to standing against the rising modernism, the chief characteristic of the fundamentalist movement was the establishment in America of the premillennial Return of Christ and the dispensational interpretation of Scripture. It was the fundamentalist movement that returned the Blessed Hope to its proper place. It further saw church planting, world missions, Jewish missions, great revival meetings, a huge contribution to our hymnology, Bible institutes, literature distribution. All of this was on an unprecedented scale, and all with the Blessed Hope at its center. And many a Baptist was a beneficiary.

There were indeed deficiencies, and as always, we have to do some sifting, but much of the best and most spiritual Bible teaching *ever*, came from that period. The authors are quick to hit out at *The Scofield Bible*. It does have problems that need to be corrected. (Back in 1985, I attempted to publish a "fixed" edition). But this Bible has helped multitudes with its succinct and spiritual presentation of Biblical truth. On balance things were probably better for Independent Baptists when they were carrying *Scofield Bibles* to church.

A massive work that appeared at the close of the fundamentalist period and gathered on to its pages much of the best of that time was Lewis Sperry Chafer's *Systematic Theology*. We certainly wish he had seen some things differently, but there is nothing on this scale nearly so good, not before him, and certainly not after. The fundamentalist literature from the Scofield to Chafer (with the Blessed Hope back at the center) was unique in the way it both instructed and edified. There needs to be some sifting, but to *flee from it* is bad advice.

If in fact there is so little in this fundamentalist period for Independent Baptists to claim for their spiritual heritage, and that we must indeed *flee from it*, can EBTS point to any other period or group that was even remotely as good (or as clear). Certainly not the Fathers, or the Reformers. Certainly not the Calvinistic, replacement theology, postmillennial, British Baptists. We do, along with later Anabaptist groups, seek to trace for our heritage that silver line of believers in the south of France and the valleys of the Piedmont who were decimated by Rome. We are convinced they were for the most part sound, we know the basics of what they taught, we know they were maligned, but there is also contradictory evidence, and we simply do not have enough of their actual teaching in our possession.

We do go back to the Bible for everything, but is there no clear historical heritage for us today? Rather than tell us to *flee from fundamentalism*, the authors of these two EBTS articles should have the grace to acknowledge that a great deal of Biblical truth was reclaimed during the fundamentalist period, and much of it a benefit to Independent Baptists. Baptists in Britain and elsewhere did not have this, in America they did. Note the difference!

The more moderate and revised form of Landmarkism as taught at EBTS, like all false teaching, soon becomes an obsession. Pastors who take this on, can talk of nothing else, every attempt must be made to "bring others on board." Discussion or fellowship soon turns to this. Other truths begin to be crowded out. I think a survey of anything connected with Landmarkism, moderate or otherwise, will show that

Premillennialism and Dispensationalism are heard of less and less. Much of the Landmark movement appears not to have believed these truths at all. EBTS is strongly premillennal, but to what extent their views affect Dispensationalism is open to question. Again, in their disparagement of the *Scofield Bible* and the large prophetic conferences of the late 1800s (p. 46), Brooks and Strouse failed to give credit for the huge impetus these gave to establishing Premillenialism in America.

On the question before us, every attempt has been made to present all of the relevant Scriptures. These have been clearly set out with emphasis. The Scripture passages have not been *imbedded* within a lot of comment. The reader can read and decide for himself without being unnecessarily distracted. When all are set out and read in a normal, natural unforced manner, the *Common View* is shown to be correct. The eleven arguments claimed for the *Revised Landmark View* are shown to break down. They cannot be *reasonably* sustained or defended. They are a manipulation rather than an exegesis of Scripture.

The Bible teaches that believers are baptised by the Holy Spirit into spiritual union with Christ. We are *in* Christ. We are *joined* to Christ. We are *members of His body, of His flesh, and of His bones* (Eph. 5:30). The outward, visible, tangible, expression of this should be the Local Church.

Jack Moorman,
London, 2007

Select Bibliography

Brooks, Ken. "Seven Fatal Flaws of Fundamentalism", *Immanuel Baptist Theological Seminary Journal,* Fall/Winter 2006.

Cambron, Mark G. *Bible Doctrines, Beliefs That Matter*, Grand Rapids: Zondervan Publishing House, 1974.

Carroll, B. H. *Ecclesia – The Church*, Ashland, Kentucky: The Baptist Examiner, n.d.

Chafer, Lewis Sperry. *Systematic Theology*, Dallas: Dallas Seminary Press, 1964.

Godsoe, Frank A. *The House of God, A Blood – Bought Body*, Del City, Oklahoma: Published by author, 1973.

Houghton, Myron J. "Baptists and the Body of Christ", *Foundation Magazine*, March-April 2003.

Huckabee, Davis W. *Studies on Church Truth*, Columbus, Georgia: Brentwood Christian Press, 1999.

Strouse, Thomas M. *I Will Build My Church, The Doctrine and History of the Baptists*, Newington, Connecticut: Emmanuel Baptist Theological Press, 2004.

_____ "EBTS Course Notes – Theology V – TH720 – Ecclesiology", Jan. 2005.

Strouse, W. Aaron. "A Critique of Historical Fundamentalism", *Immanuel Baptist Theological Seminary Journal,* Fall/Winter 2006.

Taylor, H. Boyce Sr. *Why Be a Baptist?*, Ashland, Kentucky: Ashland Avenue Baptist Publication, 1983.

Thornbury, John. *The Doctrine of the Church – A Baptist View*, Lewisburg, Pennsylvania: Heritage Publishers, 1971.

SCRIPTURES REFERENCED

INDEX

ABOUT THE AUTHOR

Dr. J. A. Moorman and his wife, Dot. 2017

Jack A. Moorman studied for a while at the Indianapolis campus of Purdue University, attended briefly Indiana Bible College, and graduated from Tennessee Temple Bible School. He has been with Baptist International Missions Inc. (BIMI) since 1967 and has been involved in church planting, Bible Institute teaching and extensive distribution of Scriptures and gospel tracts in Johannesburg, South Africa from 1968 – 1988, and in England and London since 1988. He married his wife, Dot, on November 22 1963.

J.A. Moorman has written the following scholarly books defending the King James Bible and the Hebrew, Aramaic and Greek words that underlie it:

1. When the KJV Departs from the "Majority Text."

2. Early Manuscripts, Church Fathers, and the Authorized Version.
3. Forever Settled
4. Missing in Modern Bibles—The Old Heresy Revived.
5. Samuel P. Tregelles—The Man Who Made the Critical Text Acceptable to Bible Believers.
6. 8,000 Differences Between the Textus Receptus and the Critical Text.
7. Bible Chronology: The Two Great Divides.
8. The Biblical and Observational Case for Geocentricity.

These well-documented works and are replete with evidence which he has gleaned from his own resources as well as references found in the British Museum, British Library and other libraries in South Africa and the United Kingdom.

He has been the pastor of Bethel Baptist Church in London, England since 1993. A great deal of his time, and on a nearly daily basis, is spent in distributing Gospel Literature on the crowded streets of London and beyond. May God bless his unfailing service to the Lord Jesus Christ.

www.ingramcontent.com/pod-product-compliance
Lightning Source LLC
Chambersburg PA
CBHW062008040426
42447CB00010B/1971